Pizarro, Orellana,
and the Exploration of the Amazon

General Editor

William H. Goetzmann
Jack S. Blanton, Sr., Chair in History
  University of Texas at Austin

Consulting Editor

Tom D. Crouch
Chairman, Department of Aeronautics
  National Air and Space Museum
  Smithsonian Institution

WORLD EXPLORERS

Pizarro, Orellana,
and the Exploration of the Amazon

Brendan Bernhard

Introductory Essay by Michael Collins

CHELSEA HOUSE PUBLISHERS

New York · Philadelphia

On the cover Seventeenth-century map of South America
featuring the Amazon River; portrait of Francisco Pizarro.

Chelsea House Publishers
Editor-in-Chief Remmel Nunn
Managing Editor Karyn Gullen Browne
Copy Chief Juliann Barbato
Picture Editor Adrian G. Allen
Art Director Maria Epes
Deputy Copy Chief Mark Rifkin
Assistant Art Director Noreen Romano
Series Design Loraine Machlin
Manufacturing Manager Gerald Levine
Systems Manager Lindsey Ottman
Production Manager Joseph Romano
Production Coordinator Marie Claire Cebrián

World Explorers
Senior Editor Sean Dolan

Staff for PIZARRO, ORELLANA, AND THE EXPLORATION OF THE AMAZON
Associate Editor Terrance Dolan
Copy Editor Benson D. Simmonds
Editorial Assistant Martin Mooney
Picture Researcher Nisa Rauschenberg
Senior Designer Basia Niemczyc

7 9 8 6

Library of Congress Cataloging-in-Publication Data

Bernhard, Brendan.
   Pizarro, Orellana, and the exploration of the Amazon/Brendan
Bernhard.
      p.   cm.—(World explorers)
   Includes bibliographical references and index.
   Summary: Describes the journey through the Amazon Basin made
by Orellana and Pizarro in the early sixteenth century. Also discusses
the Inca and the conquest of South America by the Spanish.
   ISBN 0-7910-1305-7
        0-7910-1529-7 (pbk.)
   1. Pizarro, Francisco, ca. 1475–1541—Juvenile literature.
2. Orellano, Francisco de, d. ca. 1546—Juvenile literature.
3. Amazon River Region—Discovery and exploration—Spanish—
Juvenile literature.   4. Explorers—South America—Biography—
Juvenile literature.   5. Explorers—Spain—Biography—Juvenile
literature. [1. Pizarro, Francisco, ca. 1475–1541. 2. Orellano,
Francisco de, d. ca. 1546. 3. Explorers. 4. Amazon River
Region—Discovery and exploration—Spanish.] I. Series.
                                                    91-9345
F3442.P776B47 1991   CIP
981'.101'0922—dc20   AC

CONTENTS

WORLD EXPLORERS

THE EARLY EXPLORERS

Herodotus and the Explorers of the Classical Age
Marco Polo and the Medieval Explorers
The Viking Explorers

THE FIRST GREAT AGE OF DISCOVERY

Jacques Cartier, Samuel de Champlain, and the Explorers of Canada
Christopher Columbus and the First Voyages to the New World
From Coronado to Escalante: The Explorers of the Spanish Southwest
Hernando de Soto and the Explorers of the American South
Sir Francis Drake and the Struggle for an Ocean Empire
Vasco da Gama and the Portuguese Explorers
La Salle and the Explorers of the Mississippi
Ferdinand Magellan and the Discovery of the World Ocean
Pizarro, Orellana, and the Exploration of the Amazon
The Search for the Northwest Passage
Giovanni da Verrazano and the Explorers of the Atlantic Coast

THE SECOND GREAT AGE OF DISCOVERY

Roald Amundsen and the Quest for the South Pole
Daniel Boone and the Opening of the Ohio Country
Captain James Cook and the Explorers of the Pacific
The Explorers of Alaska
John Charles Frémont and the Great Western Reconnaissance
Alexander von Humboldt, Colossus of Exploration
Lewis and Clark and the Route to the Pacific
Alexander Mackenzie and the Explorers of Canada
Robert Peary and the Quest for the North Pole
Zebulon Pike and the Explorers of the American Southwest
John Wesley Powell and the Great Surveys of the American West
Jedediah Smith and the Mountain Men of the American West
Henry Stanley and the European Explorers of Africa
Lt. Charles Wilkes and the Great U.S. Exploring Expedition

THE THIRD GREAT AGE OF DISCOVERY

Apollo to the Moon
The Explorers of the Undersea World
The First Men in Space
The Mission to Mars and Beyond
Probing Deep Space

CHELSEA HOUSE PUBLISHERS

Into the Unknown

Michael Collins

It is difficult to define most eras in history with any pre-cision, but not so the space age. On October 4, 1957, it burst on us with little warning when the Soviet Union launched *Sputnik*, a 184-pound cannonball that circled the globe once every 96 minutes. Less than 4 years later, the Soviets followed this first primitive satellite with the flight of Yury Gagarin, a 27-year-old fighter pilot who became the first human to orbit the earth. The Soviet Union's success prompted President John F. Kennedy to decide that the United States should "land a man on the moon and return him safely to earth" before the end of the 1960s. We now had not only a space age but a space race.

I was born in 1930, exactly the right time to allow me to participate in Project Apollo, as the U.S. lunar program came to be known. As a young man growing up, I often found myself too young to do the things I wanted—or suddenly too old, as if someone had turned a switch at midnight. But for Apollo, 1930 was the perfect year to be born, and I was very lucky. In 1966 I enjoyed circling the earth for three days, and in 1969 I flew to the moon and laughed at the sight of the tiny earth, which I could cover with my thumbnail.

How the early explorers would have loved the view from space! With one glance Christopher Columbus could have plotted his course and reassured his crew that the world was indeed round. In 90 minutes Magellan could have looked down at every port of call in the *Victoria*'s three-year circumnavigation of the globe. Given a chance to map their route from orbit, Lewis and Clark could have told President Jefferson that there was no easy Northwest Passage but that a continent of exquisite diversity awaited their scrutiny.

In a physical sense, we have already gone to most places that we can. That is not to say that there are not new adventures awaiting us deep in the sea or on the red plains of Mars, but more important than reaching new places will be understanding those we have already visited. There are vital gaps in our understanding of how our planet works as an ecosystem and how our planet fits into the infinite order of the universe. The next great age may well be the age of assimilation, in which we use microscope and telescope to evaluate what we have discovered and put that knowledge to use. The adventure of being first to reach may be replaced by the satisfaction of being first to grasp. Surely that is a form of exploration as vital to our well-being, and perhaps even survival, as the distinction of being the first to explore a specific geographical area.

The explorers whose stories are told in the books of this series did not just sail perilous seas, scale rugged mountains, traverse blistering deserts, dive to the depths of the ocean, or land on the moon. Their voyages and expeditions were journeys of mind as much as of time and distance, through which they—and all of mankind—were able to reach a greater understanding of our universe. That challenge remains, for all of us. The imperative is to see, to understand, to develop knowledge that others can use, to help nurture this planet that sustains us all. Perhaps being born in 1975 will be as lucky for a new generation of explorer as being born in 1930 was for Neil Armstrong, Buzz Aldrin, and Mike Collins.

The Reader's Journey

William H. Goetzmann

This volume is one of a series that takes us with the great explorers of the ages on bold journeys over the oceans and the continents and into outer space. As we travel along with these imaginative and courageous journeyers, we share their adventures and their knowledge. We also get a glimpse of that mysterious and inextinguishable fire that burned in the breast of men such as Magellan and Columbus—the fire that has propelled all those throughout the ages who have been driven to leave behind family and friends for a voyage into the unknown.

No one has ever satisfactorily explained the urge to explore, the drive to go to the "back of beyond." It is certain that it has been present in man almost since he began walking erect and first ventured across the African savannas. Sparks from that same fire fueled the transoceanic explorers of the Ice Age, who led their people across the vast plain that formed a land bridge between Asia and North America, and the astronauts and scientists who determined that man must reach the moon.

Besides an element of adventure, all exploration involves an element of mystery. We must not confuse exploration with discovery. Exploration is a purposeful human activity—a search for something. Discovery may be the end result of that search; it may also be an accident, as when Columbus found a whole new world while searching for the Indies. Often, the explorer may not even realize the full significance of what he has discovered, as was the case with Columbus. Exploration, on the other hand, is the product of a cultural or individual curiosity; it is a unique process that has enabled mankind to know and understand the world's oceans, continents, and polar regions. It is at the heart of scientific thinking. One of its most significant aspects is that it teaches people to ask the right questions; by doing so, it forces us to reevaluate what we think we know and understand. Thus knowledge progresses, and we are driven constantly to a new awareness and appreciation of the universe in all its infinite variety.

The motivation for exploration is not always pure. In his fascination with the new, man often forgets that others have been there before him. For example, the popular notion of the discovery of America overlooks the complex Indian civilizations that had existed there for thousands of years before the arrival of Europeans. Man's desire for conquest, riches, and fame is often linked inextricably with his quest for the unknown, but a story that touches so closely on the human essence must of necessity treat war as well as peace, avarice with generosity, both pride and humility, frailty and greatness. The story of exploration is above all a story of humanity and of man's understanding of his place in the universe.

The WORLD EXPLORERS series has been divided into four sections. The first treats the explorers of the ancient world, the Viking explorers of the 9th through the 11th centuries, and Marco Polo and the medieval explorers. The rest of the series is divided into three great ages of exploration. The first is the era of Columbus and Magellan: the period spanning the 15th and 16th centuries, which saw the discovery and exploration of the New World and the world ocean. The second might be called the age of science and imperialism, the era made possible by the scientific advances of the 17th century, which witnessed the discovery of the world's last two undiscovered continents, Australia and Antarctica, the mapping of all the continents and oceans, and the establishment of colonies all over the world. The third great age refers to the most ambitious quests of the 20th century—the probing of space and of the ocean's depths.

As we reach out into the darkness of outer space and other galaxies, we come to better understand how our ancestors confronted *oecumene*, or the vast earthly unknown. We learn once again the meaning of an unknown 18th-century sea captain's advice to navigators:

> And if by chance you make a landfall on the shores of another sea in a far country inhabited by savages and barbarians, remember you this: the greatest danger and the surest hope lies not with fires and arrows but in the quicksilver hearts of men.

At its core, exploration is a series of moral dramas. But it is these dramas, involving new lands, new people, and exotic ecosystems of staggering beauty, that make the explorers' stories not only moral tales but also some of the greatest adventure stories ever recorded. They represent the process of learning in its most expansive and vivid forms. We see that real life, past and present, transcends even the adventures of the starship *Enterprise*.

"A Thing of Awe and Amazement"

In the name of Spain and Christ they had set out to find mythical el Dorado, a city of unimaginable beauty and wealth, ruled, it was said, by a king who bathed each night in a lake of gold. *Gold*—the very mention of the word brought a light to a conquistador's eyes. How their eyes must have burned as they listened to the Indians' tales of an entire city of gold! So much of the precious stuff had been discovered by the invading Spaniards in the cities and towns of the Incas that the concept of a fabulous, golden place such as el Dorado seemed entirely possible— and even probable—to them. And if they did not find el Dorado, at the very least they were certain to find La Canela, a land of cinnamon trees they had been told about by the Indians. Gold was the ultimate prize, but cinnamon was a valuable commodity as well.

More than 200 conquistadores of the highest caliber set out for el Dorado from Quito, in present-day Ecuador, in February 1541. Added to their number were almost 200 horses; hundreds of llamas to carry supplies and to serve as food when necessary; more than 2,000 hogs to be eaten; almost as many hunting dogs; and arquebuses (large, cumbersome guns), cannons, crossbows, and other weaponry. There were also some 4,000 Indian slaves serving as guides, porters, and soldiers. At the head of this assembly strode Gonzalo Pizarro, a handsome Spanish warrior of considerable repute who was the half brother of Francisco Pizarro, the conqueror of the Incas and now the most

Spanish conquistadores arrived in force on the Pacific coast of South America in 1532 and quickly set about subduing the native inhabitants of present-day Peru and Ecuador. By 1541, Spanish expeditions into the continent's unexplored interior were under way.

powerful man in Peru. Few would have thought that such an expedition could meet with failure.

But after 11 months marked by death, sickness, and unrelenting struggle with the South American terrain, the expedition had shrunk to a fraction of its original size. The 2,000 hogs had been eaten. Some of the Indian slaves had frozen to death during the crossing of the Andes, the rugged mountain range that runs the length of western South America; some had fallen to their death in the high mountain passes or drowned in the malarial swamps of the lowlands; and almost all of the others had succumbed to fever in the rain forest and died in their chains. The Spaniards had encountered no wealthy communities to plunder and take possession of, had founded no colonies, and in 11 months had hacked their way through a mere 200 miles of jungle, a seemingly futile and endless labor. El Dorado was now a dream that even the dreamers no longer believed in, and the cinnamon trees they had found were of poor quality and pitifully scarce. An enraged Pizarro began torturing the remaining Indians. Some were burned to death; others were fed alive to the ravenous dogs.

Starving, exhausted, feverish, and filthy; their armor rusting in the jungle humidity and their beards matted and lice ridden; plagued by insects, spiders, scorpions, snakes, and vampire bats, the Spaniards came to a halt in December 1541 near the headwaters of Ecuador's Napo River. Many of these men had been part of the tiny army of conquistadores that had destroyed the great Inca nation, but the bold Spaniards who had subdued one of the greatest empires on earth could not subdue the lands that had hosted that empire, and now they were on the brink of extinction themselves.

A one-eyed conquistador named Francisco de Orellana stepped forward and offered to lead an advance party to scout for food and friendly Indian villages. Pizarro gave him leave to do so, for the 30-year-old Orellana was a trusted friend and a reliable lieutenant, and he promised

to return within 10 or 12 days at most. He would take the expedition's one sizable boat and more than a quarter of the men, including a Dominican friar, Gaspar de Carvajal. He would also take three arquebuses, gunpowder, five crossbows, and a number of canoes. Orellana bade farewell to Pizarro on December 26, 1541, and set off down the Napo. He would never see Gonzalo Pizarro again, but ironically this leave-taking was to permanently link the names Pizarro and Orellana. It would also cast a shadow over the subsequent accomplishments of Orellana.

Visions of the fabled golden city of el Dorado beckoned to Spanish adventurers in both North and South America in the 16th and 17th centuries. Conquistador Gonzalo Pizarro marched into the Amazon rain forest on a doomed quest for el Dorado in February 1541.

The Spaniards forced thousands of Indian slaves to serve as porters during the el Dorado expedition. According to Bartolomé de Las Casas—the so-called Apostle to the Indies, the first priest ordained in the New World, and a staunch critic of Spanish mistreatment of the Indians—"When one of the wretched, overladen Indians broke down from sheer exhaustion, his head was immediately chopped off, and the burden heaped upon another."

On December 27, near the riverbank, Orellana's boat struck a submerged tree trunk, which punched a large hole in the floor of the vessel and nearly sank it. Once the boat had been repaired the Spaniards moved out into the middle of the river to avoid any more accidents. There, the current was considerably stronger. They flew downriver at a great pace without seeing any sign of inhabited land or food of any kind. Having spent almost a year hacking through the jungle at a snail's pace, the conquistadores must have found the speed at which they now traveled both exhilarating and alarming. Already doubts were beginning to creep into their minds about the feasibility of returning to Pizarro. Should they turn back now, before it was too late to do so?

They had now gone three days without food. The river was inexorable, pulling them steadily along. An impenetrable and forbidding wall of jungle lay on either side, endless and seemingly uninhabited. They began to hear drums but concluded that the sound was an auditory hallucination brought on by malnutrition. A week went by and hunger turned to delirium. Father Carvajal, who was to become the chronicler of Orellana's journey, recalled the deplorable condition of the Spaniards as they went ashore to forage: "We reached a state of privation so great that we were eating nothing but leather, belts, and soles of shoes, cooked with certain herbs, with the result that so great was our weakness that we could not remain standing, for some on all fours and others with staffs went off into the woods to search for a few roots to eat and some there were who ate certain herbs with which they were not familiar, and they were at the point of death [and] they were like mad men and did not possess sense."

Back on the river, they began to hear drums again but this time they were real, and several canoes full of Indians appeared. The Indians rowed out to inspect the strange boat, for it was of a shape and size they had never seen before, and it was overflowing with equally strange men. Despite their weakened condition, Orellana's company managed to act in a sufficiently threatening manner, and the Indians turned around and headed for the shore and the safety of their village. Orellana ordered his men to row directly for the village, and the frightened Indians disappeared into the jungle. The Spaniards went ashore and explored the deserted town. There was food here, and plenty of it. In the houses of this village, according to Carvajal, Orellana's men "set about to make up for the past, because they did nothing but eat of that which the Indians had prepared for themselves and drink of their beverages, and this they did with so much eagerness that they thought that they would never satisfy themselves."

The famished Spaniards did manage to satisfy themselves—for a month. Orellana, who had studied the languages of the South American Indians, was far more adept in matters of diplomacy than Pizarro, and he quickly set about befriending the Indians whose food they had just eaten. He conversed with the Indians, informing them that he wished them no harm, and learned that this was the village of Imara, ruled by the chief Aparia the Lesser. Orellana asked to speak with the chief, the subsequent meeting went well, and the guests were officially welcomed. Orellana presented his host with what modest gifts he could muster, and when gifts were offered in return, the conquistador was quick to put in a request for food. Within hours, he and his men were presented with an abundance of "meats, partridges, turkeys and fish of many sorts."

The Spaniards stayed in Imara for a month, eating, drinking, resting, and contemplating what to do next. Should they attempt to return upriver to Pizarro? From the Indians, Orellana learned that he was now an astonishing 700 miles from Pizarro's camp—more than 3 times the distance they had managed to travel in all of the previous year. Furthermore, he now knew beyond doubt that the intervening region was uninhabited and devoid of food. And the current that had borne them downriver so swiftly would now hinder their progress back upriver. It might take months to travel the same distance, and they could not possibly take enough food to last them that long. Even

Failing to find el Dorado, and believing that the Indians knew where it was but were withholding the information, Gonzalo Pizarro began burning them alive.

if they did manage to survive such a journey, it seemed unlikely that Pizarro would wait for them.

It was clear to Orellana that to go back was out of the question. His men agreed, and they made their feelings plain in a formal, written petition, begging their leader, "In the name of God and of the King . . . not to enter on this so up-hill journey, in which the lives of so many able-bodied men are placed in jeopardy . . . and let not Your Worship take the position of ordering us to do so, for that will be furnishing an occasion for our disobeying Your Worship."

The conquistadores took to the river once again. The current continued to grow stronger, and some of the Spaniards began to fear that they were being sucked downstream toward some calamity. They could hear a great roaring up ahead, and it grew louder each day. Finally they came to the place where the Napo was absorbed by another, truly monstrous river. They were appalled by the size and power of this new river. According to Friar Carvajal, "It [the new river] did away with and completely mastered the other [Napo] river, and it seemed as if it swallowed it up within itself, because it came on with such fury and with so great an onrush that it was a thing of much awe and amazement to see such a jam of trees and dead timber as it brought along with it, such that it was enough to fill one with the greatest fear just to look at it, let alone to go through it."

Orellana and his small troop of conquistadores had come to the junction of the Napo and the greatest river in the world—the Amazon. The Amazon's irresistible current, if they chose to continue, would carry them into the interior of South America and through a rain forest so huge it dwarfed their native Spain. They would be the first Europeans to penetrate this mysterious tropical wilderness. If any of them still harbored thoughts of turning back, this was truly the last chance they would have to do so. But they were conquistadores, and turning back was against their nature.

The Ransom of Atahualpa

Christopher Columbus, who discovered the Americas in 1492; Vincente Yáñez Pinzón, who in 1500 explored the coast of Brazil and discovered the mouth of the giant river that would be investigated more fully by Orellana; Juan Ponce de León, who began the conquest of Puerto Rico in 1508 and discovered Florida five years later; Diego Velázquez, who founded the city of Havana, Cuba, in 1515; Vasco Núñez de Balboa, who in 1513 became the first European to see the Pacific Ocean; Francisco Férnandez de Córdoba, who in 1517 discovered Mexico's Yucatán peninsula; Ferdinand Magellan, who spent three years from 1519 to 1522 circumnavigating the world; Hernán Cortés, who invaded Mexico in 1518 and conquered the Aztec empire.

These were some of the more famous conquistadores to precede the Pizarros and Orellana. Theirs is a tale of improbable exploits and impossible victories; for sheer audacity in the face of overwhelming peril, history has yet to provide their equal. They were the shock troops of the Spanish conquest, men who lived extraordinary lives during an extraordinary period in Spanish and New World history. Their arrogance was almost godlike, and indeed, they were often thought to be gods by the peoples, such as Mexico's Aztecs, whom they subdued. This arrogance frequently manifested itself in acts of great cruelty. As

Heavily armored soldiers—never before encountered by the native South Americans—represented the vanguard of the Spanish conquest. With combat skills that matched the superiority of their weaponry, the conquistadores wreaked havoc on the Indians of the New World.

Christians and as Spanish soldiers they lived in the conviction that they were doubly blessed—both history and God were on their side. They were part of the mightiest army in the world, a fighting force honed to perfection during the wars with the fierce Muslim armies they had driven from Spain; and they were also Christian crusaders, bringing the word of Christ to "heathen" and "barbaric" civilizations. And if their arrogance was monumental, so

Conquistador Vincente Yáñez Pinzón was the first European to see the Amazon River. While exploring the coast of Brazil in 1500, Pinzón came upon the place where the gigantic river empties itself into the Atlantic.

was their greed. Hernán Cortés, one of the greatest—and cruelest—of all the conquistadores, remarked that "we Spanish suffer from a disease of the heart which can be cured only by gold."

In 1527, Spanish ships—one of them captained by Francisco Pizarro—exploring the Pacific coast of South America encountered, off the coast of Ecuador, a balsa raft carrying 20 Inca Indians. This was the first contact between two great militaristic empires—the empire of King Charles I of Spain and the empire of Inca Atahualpa of Peru (*Inca* was the title given to the absolute overlord of the empire as well as to the people of the empire). The Spaniards took the Indians prisoner, interrogated them and examined their craft and their goods. "They were carrying many pieces of silver and gold as personal ornaments," the Spaniards wrote with palpable excitement in their report to the king. "[The Indians had] crowns and diadems, belts and bracelets, armour for the legs and breastplates; tweezers and rattles and strings and clusters of beads and rubies; mirrors decorated with silver, and cups and other drinking vessels. They were carrying many wool and cotton mantles and Moorish tunics . . . and other pieces of clothing coloured with cochineal, crimson, blue, yellow and all other colours, and worked with different types of ornate embroidery, in figures of birds, animals, fish and trees. They had some tiny weights to weigh gold. There were small stones in bead bags: emeralds and chalcedonies and other jewels and pieces of crystal and resin."

Visions of conquest and plunder danced before the Spaniards' eyes. Every conquistador and would-be conquistador in Spain ached to be the next Hernán Cortés: In 1518, with an army of only 600 men, Cortés had invaded and conquered the powerful Aztec empire of Mexico, acquiring glory and fabulous riches in the process. Word of the encounter with the Inca seamen spread, and by 1530, after leading two reconnaissance expeditions along the coast of Peru, Francisco Pizarro had received permission from the king to organize a full-scale expedition of conquest. Among the conquistadores who joined the expedition was Pizarro's younger brother Gonzalo, from the town of Trujillo. A teenage contemporary of Gonzalo's, Francisco de Orellana, also from Trujillo, had sailed with one of the earlier sorties and was waiting in Panama with other conquistadores for the arrival of the main force of invasion.

In September 1532, at the head of a column of about 160 Spaniards, Francisco Pizarro began his march into Peru. Moving inland and southward, Pizarro led his force toward the heart of the Inca empire—the city of Cuzco, located high in the Peruvian Andes. What followed was one of the most shocking military campaigns in history. An observer who was aware of the size and strength of the Inca empire would have concluded immediately that the conquistadores were marching to their death, for the *Tawantinsuyu*, the Inca name for the empire, was no loose conglomeration of primitive tribes.

Stretching for 3,000 miles along the Andes, from central Chile to southern Colombia, and comprising 20 million people, the Tawantinsuyu was a sophisticated, acutely centralized, militaristic empire. From Cuzco, the original Incas had expanded outward, conquering and assimilating the various peoples of Chile, Peru, Ecuador, Colombia, and parts of Brazil. Inca engineers and architects built cities, fortresses, aquaducts, and temples on the Andean slopes; great highways, better than even the famed roads of the Romans, connected all parts of the far-flung empire; skilled artisans wrought gold and silver into gorgeous shapes; and huge professional armies continued the expansion of the realm. The Incas worshiped the sun, and Inca economy and society was based on a highly organized system of collective farming. Private property was forbidden, crime was nonexistent, and perhaps most remarkable of all, none of the 20 million subjects of the Tawantinsuyu ever went hungry.

These facts make the ensuing events all the more extraordinary. Pizarro marched his small army up into the mountains to Cajamarca, where the Inca himself, Atahualpa, was encamped with one of his armies. On Saturday, November 16, 1532, Atahualpa, with several thousand warriors, and Pizarro, with his 160 conquistadores, confronted each other in the town square. The Spaniards launched a surprise attack. They discharged their cannons, arquebuses, and crossbows, and, wielding swords and lances, charged their horses into the midst of the Indians. Two hours of slaughter followed. When it

Hernán Cortés and his fellow conquistadores wage war on the army of Aztec emperor Montezuma in 1518. His success in conquering the Aztec, and the renown and wealth he enjoyed as a result, spurred many of his fellow Estremadurans—including the Pizarros and Francisco de Orellana—to undertake similar adventures.

Francisco Pizarro, first governor of Peru. Pizarro was at the head of the tiny invasion force that hacked its way through the Inca empire in 1532. His younger brother, Gonzalo, and Orellana participated in the invasion as well.

was over, 2,000 butchered Incas lay in heaps in the square; 5,000 others sat moaning in the square or wandered about in shock, suffering from grievous injuries. The rest of Atahualpa's once-proud army had fled. Atahualpa himself was taken prisoner by the Spaniards. None of the Spaniards were killed in the "fight," and only one of them sustained an injury.

The Cajamarca massacre signaled the beginning of the end of the Inca empire. And, astonishing as it seems, it was a scene that was to be repeated again and again as the Spaniards continued the conquest of Peru, marching inexorably southward through the Andes along the Inca royal road to Cuzco, which they entered and sacked in November 1533. For centuries, historians have been asking the same question: How did a mere 160 Spaniards bring an entire empire to its knees? There are several answers to this question. Individually, none of them seem sufficient to explain the fall of the Tawantinsuyu. But taken together, they provide at least the basis of an explanation.

Pizarro's timing was perfect. Five years had elapsed between the first encounter with the Incas in 1527 and the capture of Inca Atahualpa in 1532. During those five years, the previous Inca had died and a bitter struggle for the throne among his offspring had turned into a destructive civil war. Pizarro arrived in Peru just after Atahualpa had defeated his brother's armies and taken control of the country. Thus the conquistadores invaded a weakened empire, for the civil war had had a debilitating effect that helped undermine its former inner cohesion.

An element of cultural as well as military surprise played a crucial role. The Incas had never seen Europeans before. Nor had they seen horses. Cut off by the Amazon rain forest on one side and by an ocean on the other, Incan civilization had developed in complete isolation. They were as little prepared for the sight of the Spaniards and their horses as we would be for aliens from outer space. These large, pale-skinned, hairy beings, covered from head to toe in shining armor, riding monstrous, galloping, snorting beasts (like the Aztecs, many of the Incas believed horse and conquistador to be a single creature), frightened the Indians by their very appearance. The weapons the Spaniards used, along with the sheer ferocity of their attack, turned fright to outright panic. The arquebuses flashed, roared, and belched smoke at the Indians; the crossbows were accurate and deadly; and the battle-hardened Spaniards hacked with their long steel swords and stabbed with their cruel lances. The horses especially gave the Spaniards the decisive edge in any stand-up confrontation with the Indians. The Inca warriors, who were, in effect, fighting with Bronze Age weapons—clubs, sticks,

Conquistadores attack the massive army of Inca Atahualpa at Cajamarca, Peru, November 16, 1532. Badly outnumbered, the Spaniards nevertheless routed the Indians and captured Atahualpa.

flimsy wooden spears and arrows—had as little chance
against the heavily armored, mounted Spaniards as the
Polish cavalry had against Hitler's panzer tanks at the beginning of World War II.   *(continued on page 32)*

The Inca Royal Road

The conquistadores who invaded the mountainous Inca empire in 1531 found a country where the ingenuity of the inhabitants had combined with the overwhelmingly beautiful—and terrible—natural environment to form a place of wonders, a kingdom in the clouds. The towns and cities of the empire were strewn along the massive Andes cordillera, cradled in breathtaking valleys or clinging to the towering mountains. As the Spanish adventurers marched toward the capital city of Cuzco, they saw with admiring eyes the results of the Incas' extraordinary talent for engineering and architecture.

The Europeans were particularly impressed by the stonework of the Inca masons. Although they lacked any kind of mortar, the Incas built walls stronger than the Spaniards themselves were able to build. Using stones of irregular shapes, the Indian masons laid rock upon rock with such precision that they all fit together snugly, like pieces of an elaborate puzzle. Many of these walls still stand today, whereas those built by the Spaniards have succumbed to the elements, earthquakes, and decay.

Most impressive of all was the Inca royal road. Stretching for almost 2,000 miles over, around, and through the Andes chain, the stone highway connected the cities and towns of the Inca empire, from Caranquí (in present-day Colombia) in the north to Copiapó (in present-day Chile) in the south. Smaller lateral roads branched off the main highway toward the towns on the coast and those farther inland. The royal road was made of flagstone paving supported by sturdy stone embankments. At some places it became a zigzagging stairway consisting of hundreds of thousands of steps leading up the mountains into the clouds or down into the deep Andean gorges. Harrowing rope bridges that were actually very reliable allowed travelers to cross the rivers that roared along the deep canyons, and sometimes the highway tunneled right through the rock itself, disappearing into the mountainside only to reappear farther on.

The Inca royal road was perhaps the single most important feature in the maintenance of the empire's social and political cohesion, transforming a virtually impassable region into a well-traveled thorough-fare and allowing commerce to flourish and information to travel easily between the king-dom's far-flung cities. Upon seeing the great stone highway for the first time, conquistador Hernando Pizarro wrote that "such magnificent roads could be seen no-where in Christendom."

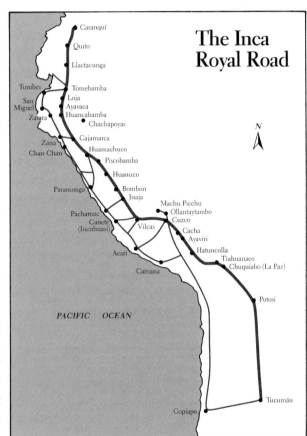

The Inca Royal Road

Caranquí
Quito
Llactacunga
Tumbes
Tomebamba
San Miguel
Loja
Ayavaca
Zarara
Huancabamba
Chachapoyas
Cajamarca
Zana
Huamachuco
Chan Chan
Piscobamba
Huanuco
Paramonga
Bombon
Juaja
Machu Picchu
Ollantaytambo
Pachamac
Cuzco
Canete
(Incuhuasi)
Vilcas
Cacha
Ayaviri
Acari
Hatuncolla
Tiahuanaco
Camana
Chuquiabo (La Paz)
Potosi
PACIFIC OCEAN
Tucumán
Copiapo

N

Pizarro's army carried the war deep into the Inca empire, eventually reaching the capital city, Cuzco, which was sacked and burned in November 1533. The Spaniards found more gold in Cuzco than in any other Inca city.

(continued from page 29)

The element of surprise and military superiority accounts for the events at Cajamarca and the Spaniards' initial victories along the royal road to Cuzco. Even so, would not the sheer disparity in numbers—in that first year of the invasion, even with reinforcements trickling in, the Spanish army never numbered more than about 200—allow the Incas to eventually crush the Spaniards? Would not the empire's population of 20 million stir, and like one of the monstrous anacondas of South America envelop the invaders in its great coils and smother them?

If Pizarro had not captured Atahualpa at Cajamarca, the answer to this question would have been yes. But in taking the ruler captive, Pizarro succeeded in cutting off the anaconda's head.

To understand the effect that Atahualpa's capture had on the Inca empire one must understand Inca society and the role an overlord such as Atahualpa played in it. Peruvian novelist Mario Vargas Llosa has addressed this issue in an essay entitled "Questions of Conquest." Llosa writes of the Tawantinsuyu that "the individual had no importance and virtually no existence in that pyramidal and theocratic society whose achievements had always been collective and anonymous. . . . A state religion that took away the individual's free will and crowned the authority's decisions with the aura of a divine mandate turned the Tawantinsuyu into a beehive—laborious, efficient, stoic. But its immense power was in fact, very fragile. . . . As soon as the Inca, that figure who was the . . . axis around which the entire society was organized and upon which depended the life and death of every person, from the richest to the poorest, was captured, no one knew how to act. . . . When, after the initial confusion, attempts to resist started breaking out here and there, it was too late. . . . Leaderless . . . the Inca system seems to fall into a monumental state of confusion."

In desperation, and having already noticed the Spaniards' appetite for gold, Atahualpa attempted to buy his freedom. As ransom, he promised to fill with gold the room in Cajamarca where he was held captive. The room was 22 feet long, 17 feet wide, and 9 feet high. Although the Spaniards had no intention of releasing Atahualpa, they accepted his offer. Gold began pouring in from all parts of the empire as the populace attempted to ransom Atahualpa; gold in fantastic shapes and staggering quantities; gold beyond the wildest dreams of any conquistador! In the meantime, on their own initiative, the Spaniards were plundering the gold-filled cities and temples of the

realm. More than 11 tons of gold arrived in Cajamarca
during the first year and a half of the conquest; gold in
the form of dishes, vases, icons, jewelry, baubles, ornaments. In Cuzco, the Spaniards came upon the Temple
of the Sun and within it the legendary Golden Enclosure,
Coricancha. Here, there were life-size golden sentries and
llamas, as well as golden icons and ceremonial pitchers
and jars of gold. And most amazing of all was the artificial
garden made entirely of gold—the fountains, the trees,
the flowers, the birds, the grass, even the insects, were
golden.

All of these beautiful objects, the result of the labors of
generations of gifted Inca goldsmiths, were brought to Cajamarca, where they were fed into huge fires, melted down
into bars, and stamped with the Spanish royal seal. Atahualpa's ransom was never completed—although an es-
timated $6 million worth of gold was deposited in his
room—because on July 26, 1533, Pizarro, deciding that
the Inca had outlived his usefulness, had him put to death.
A puppet Inca, answerable to Pizarro, was installed. The
Tawantinsuyu went into a swift and irreversible decline.
The number of Spanish troops in Peru steadily increased.
Among the Indians, animosity from their civil war lin-
gered, and like Cortés in Mexico, Pizarro played one side
off against the other in order to prevent them from mount-
ing a united resistance against the Spaniards. Peru became
a hellish place, a land dominated by war, greed, and
oppression. Those Spaniards who had arrived after the
initial two years of the conquest came too late to share in
the fantastic wealth that had fallen into the laps of the first
invaders, and Francisco Pizarro had to find other ways of
keeping the boisterous conquistadores happy. This was
done by granting each of them the rights to a section of
land and a generous number of Indian slaves. Thus the
great empire was divided up and parceled out to an ever-
growing number of Spaniards. Inevitably, war broke out

among the Spaniards themselves as they jealously disputed the administration of their new dominion. In this brutal and treacherous environment, Francisco de Orellana and Gonzalo Pizarro came of age.

Inca Atahualpa watches from the doorway of his prison room in Cajamarca as his subjects bring golden objects for his ransom.

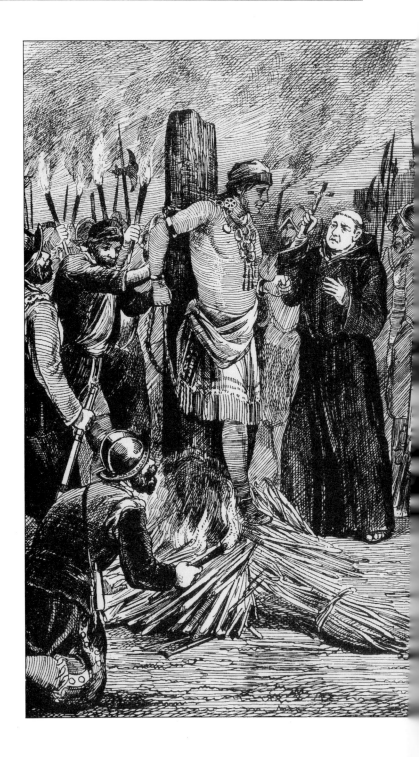

A Catholic priest baptizes Inca Atahualpa moments before his execution in the Cajamarca town square on July 26, 1533. A witness recalled that upon the Inca's death, "all the native populace who were in the square . . . prostrated themselves on the ground, letting themselves fall to the earth like drunken men."

The Golden Man

By 1541 the supremacy of the Spanish in Peru had been securely established, and the conquistadores had even indulged in the luxury of a civil war, in which Orellana had faithfully fought (losing an eye in the process) on the side of the Pizarros, who were victorious. Orellana and Gonzalo Pizarro had done well for themselves in the decade of turmoil that followed the invasion of Peru. Both young men established reputations as important conquistadores. Orellana founded the city of Santiago de Guayaquil and was appointed captain general and then lieutenant governor of the city of Puertoviejo by Francisco Pizarro as a reward for his faithful service in the civil war. Gonzalo Pizarro, however, had already bypassed his former townsman on the ladder of the Spanish colonial hierarchy, having been named governor of the entire province of Quito. Although Gonzalo was younger than Orellana, he was clearly the more renowned, partly because his achievements were of a more sensational nature than Orellana's— Gonzalo was a fierce warrior and an expert horseman— and partly because he was the half brother of Francisco Pizarro, the conqueror and now governor of Peru.

Orellana was something of an anomaly among conquistadores. He won his reputation not by notable success on the battlefield—although he was no coward—but rather by intelligence, loyalty, and hard work. By temperament, he was as much an administrator as a soldier, and he had

In Cuzco in 1535, rival conquistadores Francisco Pizarro (left) and Diego de Almagro the Elder (right) swear a truce between their two factions. Tensions between the Almagrists and the Pizarros continued nevertheless, civil war broke out, and in 1538, Hernando Pizarro defeated the Almagrist forces in a battle outside Cuzco. Almagro the Elder was captured and garroted.

a gift for languages. Few, if any conquistadores of the time could claim to be brilliant linguists, as Orellana was acknowledged to be by all who knew him. In fact, most of the conquistadores were illiterate. Orellana, on the other hand, systematically studied the various Indian dialects he encountered and even made small vocabulary primers for each. This clearly set him apart from his comrades. He was also an evenhanded and effective administrator—a rarity among conquistadores. The city councillors of Santiago de Guayaquil attested to this in a letter to King Charles, stating that Orellana was a person "capable of, and qualified for, whatever commissions and offices His Majesty might be pleased to intrust to him, be it a governorship or any others whatsoever, because he is a person who would give a good account of them."

One thing that Orellana and Gonzalo Pizarro (and all the conquistadores) did have in common was inexhaustible ambition. ("The lust for glory extends beyond this mortal life, and taking a whole world will hardly satisfy it, much less one or two kingdoms," Cortés had written.) Despite their success in the New World, the old hunger still burned within, and neither was satisfied or ready to rest on his laurels. Gonzalo aspired to be the equal of his half brother Francisco—to discover new lands and new cultures, and then to conquer them for Spain. Orellana's chief ambition was to be the governor of a province, as Gonzalo was. The path to such a power, however, lay not in linguistic and administrative aptitude but in exploration and conquest.

Given their unbridled ambition and their appetite for gold, it is not surprising that the persistent rumors the Spaniards heard about a land to the east called el Dorado (the Golden Man) should have taken hold of their imagination. Nor is it surprising that these supposedly sophisticated Europeans actually believed such tall tales, for they had already seen incredible things. Some of the older soldiers were veterans of Cortés's conquest of the fabulous Aztec empire. Others had participated in the sack of the

Inca capital of Cuzco. After the crowning of a new Inca in Cuzco the Spaniards had seen women hold out their hands for the Inca to spit into when he wanted to spit, and they had watched, in awe, as the city's entire population got drunk for days, until the drains that bisected every street flooded with accumulated urine. Some had witnessed one of the last great Inca royal hunts, in which 10,000 Indians took part, driving deer, foxes, hares, and even pumas down from the hills into the valleys, where, forced into a shrinking circle by the men who surrounded them, 11,000 animals were slaughtered. And any conquistador who had seen with his own eyes the glittering

The Muysca Indians of Peru engage in the ceremony that probably inspired the myth of el Dorado, where a "golden man" supposedly ruled over a golden city. The Indians honored a new chieftain by anointing his body with balsam and then blowing gold dust onto him, thus creating a kind of golden man.

The massive Andes Cordillera forms a rugged natural boundary between South America's Pacific coast and the continental interior. During Gonzalo Pizarro's trek inland, many of the Indian slaves froze to death in the high mountain passes.

wonders of the Golden Enclosure could not discount the possibility of an el Dorado. (The legend of el Dorado seems to have originated with Peru's Muysca Indians, who would cover a new chief with sticky resin and then sprinkle gold dust over the resin, creating, in effect, a golden man. The chief would then bathe in a sacred lake while his people tossed emeralds and gold into the water in tribute.)

As soon as Gonzalo Pizarro announced his intention to mount an expedition to el Dorado, Orellana traveled from Puertoviejo to Quito and requested permission to participate. After he obtained Pizarro's approval, Orellana hurried back home; it was obvious to him that Pizarro was eager to start out as soon as possible, and Orellana had a

great deal to do in a short time. Orellana had assured
Pizarro that he intended to bring with him a sizable group
of conquistadores who would be a credit to so great an
expedition. These he selected from his own followers in
Puertoviejo and Santiago de Guayaquil. He also had to
make sure that those towns, for which he would remain
responsible, would be well governed after his departure.
In the end he chose 20 men to accompany him on the
expedition and spent the lavish sum of 40,000 pesos to
equip them as fully as possible. Most of the money was
spent on horses, which were extraordinarily expensive; all
the horses in Peru had either been imported from Spain
(only one in two generally survived the two-month ocean
voyage) or bought from horse traders from Cuba or Ja-
maica.

Orellana and his retinue arrived in Quito on March 11,
1541, only to be told that Gonzalo Pizarro had already
left. To the Quitans who gave him the bad news—and
who had already seen Pizarro set out at the head of a
tremendous parade of conquistadores, slaves, and animals—Orellana's crew must have looked pitifully small,
and they advised him against an attempt to catch up with
Pizarro, who had gotten a considerable head start. The
journey would be too dangerous, Orellana was told. The
country they would be passing through was exceedingly
rough and mountainous. There was snow on the peaks
just seven miles outside Quito. Furthermore, his small
force of men would be at the mercy of hostile Indians in
that part of the country.

But Orellana was determined to press on. The march
across the cordillera to Pizarro's camp in the valley of
Zumaco took several weeks and was as hard and dangerous
as the people of Quito had predicted. Pizarro's immense
entourage had stripped the country of food and had badly
alienated the natives who, seeing Orellana's weary gang
as more of the same, attacked them with vigor at every
opportunity. Orellana and his men fought them off and

kept going. By the time they entered the Zumaco Valley, the condition of Orellana's men had become so bad that he was forced to send word of his desperate situation ahead to Pizarro's camp. Pizarro's reply was prompt: Soldiers were immediately sent to bring food to Orellana's starving party and to help them complete the last leg of the journey. When they at last arrived at Pizarro's camp, Orellana and his men were in an utterly bedraggled state. But Pizarro greeted Orellana warmly, congratulated him on his tenacity, and on the spot appointed him second-in-command with the rank of lieutenant general.

The Spaniards spent the next nine months hacking their way through the dense rain forest in a fruitless search for el Dorado or the great cinnamon tree groves of which the Indians had spoken. Eventually they gave up the quest for these chimeras and simply concentrated on finding food and staying alive. By December 1541 many of the Spaniards had died and almost all of those who still lived were sick. Thus, when Orellana offered to take a scouting party down the Napo to search for food, Pizarro gratefully gave him his blessing. A week later, Orellana and his men were happily ensconced in the village of Imara.

They spent a month in Imara, the village ruled by Aparia the Lesser. Good food was available on a daily basis (although seven of the Spaniards never recovered from the starvation they had endured and died in Imara). According to Friar Carvajal, "The Mercy of God permitted the Indians from the districts round about that stopping-place to come in a peaceful mood, and just like friends some gave us fish in exchange for barter goods, others brought in birds and a certain quantity of monkey-cat meat; and in that village this worn-out company of ours got a rest, not only those who were sick, but those who were well."

Once the Spaniards had decided to continue down the river instead of making an attempt to return to Pizarro, preparations had to be made for the voyage. The Spaniards were of the unanimous opinion that a new brigantine (a

two-masted square-rigged ship) should be built, but this
was easier said than done. They were stranded in the jungle
with virtually no materials for such a task, and none of
them were shipbuilders. This was the type of situation in
which the conquistadores excelled, however. Friar Carvajal described the effort to produce the supplies they
would need to build the vessel: "There being no craftsmen

*In December 1541, Pizarro's
expedition came upon the Napo
River. The Napo's waters originate
on volcanic Mount Cotopaxi, in
present-day Ecuador, and flow for
550 miles, eventually emptying
into the Amazon River.*

who were expert in this or that trade, some were engaged in making charcoal in spite of their not being charcoal burners, others in cutting and bringing in wood in spite of their not being woodcutters, others making nails in spite of their not being smiths, and others in working the bellows of the forge; and . . . within a few days two thousand nails of good quality were made out of the chains and horseshoes and iron materials which were found scattered among the company."

Orellana and his men encountered friendly Indians at Imara, a village situated on the banks of the Napo River. The citizens of Imara fed the starving Spaniards and allowed them to rest in their village for a month before they resumed their journey downriver.

The Spaniards did not stay in Imara to begin construction of the vessel itself, however. Fifty hungry conquistadores proved to be costly and noisy guests. They had worn out their welcome, and a notable cooling in relations with the villagers set in. The daily visits and food baskets were no longer forthcoming. The conquistadores loaded as much food as they could still obtain, as well as the material for the new vessel, onto their boat and their canoes and took to the river again.

For the next three weeks on the river the Spaniards passed through "many hardships and very extraordinary dangers." They had planned to stop in a village farther on down the Napo after its chief had visited them in Imara and extended an invitation. They were unable to do so, however, because of the conjunction of another river with the Napo at that point. The water was so rough, and the current sent so many dead tree trunks hurtling downstream that they were barely able to keep their shaky craft afloat. Having been forced to miss one of the few invitations that they were ever to receive, the Spaniards now passed only burned villages (the result of tribal warfare) and uninhabited land. Supplies began to run low again.

During a break for fishing, 11 men in 2 canoes got lost among some islands and were separated from the main party. They were reunited 2 days later, to the joy and relief of all, for the loss of 11 men would have been a serious blow to the party's chances of surviving the river journey. Orellana had already been informed by the Indians of Imara of the fierce tribes they could expect to meet, including those ruled by great warlords, such as Machiparo, Omagua, and Paguana. Expect a hostile reception, the Spaniards had been told. Greatly outnumbered as they were, they could not afford to lose any more men. As a result, Orellana commanded that no one stray more than a crossbow shot's distance from the main party. The company would soon find out that this was a wise decision.

Machiparo's Domain

On February 11, 1542, the conquistadores reached the Amazon. They decided to trust their fate to the river, which quickly took hold of their flimsy little ship and drew it into the heart of the continent. The Spaniards had no way of knowing the true length and size of the river and thus the scope of the journey that lay before them; had they known, no doubt they would have been appalled.

The Amazon is the world's largest river. Although the Nile River is longer, it does not carry the huge volume of water that the Amazon does. The Amazon is almost 4,000 miles long and discharges 60 times the amount of water the Nile discharges (one-fifth of all the fresh water that flows into the earth's oceans comes from the Amazon). Originating in the Peruvian Andes, the Amazon snakes across the continent from west to east and empties into the Atlantic, near present-day Belém, Brazil. The river has as many as 500 tributaries and is 50 miles wide at some points.

The Amazon River is the main artery of the world's largest tropical rain forest, a jungle so immense it could swallow continental Australia. Orellana and his companions were about to plunge into the depths of this ecosystem, and they would find that it is primarily a place of riotous, unchecked *growth* of every imaginable—and to the Spaniards up to this point unimaginable—form of life. In the face of such overwhelming fecundity even a conquistador might feel insignificant.

By February 1542, Orellana's river-bound conquistadores had been drawn into the depths of the Amazon rain forest. They marveled at the lush ecosystem and the abundance and variety of life it supported, but the Europeans had difficulty adapting to their new environment and behaved more like plunderers than explorers.

In a single square mile of Amazonian rain forest more than 3,000 separate types of plants can be found. These plants provide one-third of the earth's oxygen. Edible tropical fruits are plentiful. The rain forest also hosts an astounding variety of wildlife. Jaguars, many different kinds of monkeys, sloths, anteaters, deer, armadillos, peccaries, tapirs, capybaras (the world's largest rodent), snakes (lethal and nonlethal, from tiny to truly monstrous), vampire bats, and giant fruit bats are but a few of the many species to be found in the Amazon rain forest. Almost 2,000 species of birds live in and around the jungle's canopy.

Insects and spiders, many of which the conquistadores would get to know on an uncomfortably intimate basis—the Amazon is home to one-third of the earth's million species of insects—thrive in the rain forest. There are killer bees, army ants, scorpions, tarantulas, centipedes, ticks, flies, clouds of mosquitoes, and a multitude of different types of butterflies, almost all of them startling in their beauty.

The river itself teems with life; 2,500 different species of fish swim in its waters, including flesh-gobbling piranhas, electric eels, stingrays, silver carp, neon tetras, the giant catfish, and the giant redfish (the world's largest freshwater fish, growing up to 600 pounds and 15 feet in length). Manatees (sea cows), which are almost extinct today, provoked a lively debate among the Spaniards over whether the creature was a fish or a mammal (it is a mammal) and therefore whether it could be eaten on Fridays (Roman Catholics abstained from eating meat on Fridays). The manatee grows up to 8 feet in length and can weigh as much as 2,000 pounds. Among the manatees' neighbors are giant river otters, caimans, crocodiles, freshwater dolphins, frogs, toads, and turtles. The Indians and the Spaniards found turtle meat to be delicious; the Indians often kept them in large, partially submerged enclosures on the river in front of their villages, a practice the Spaniards would take advantage of during their journey.

The Amazon

It seems odd that while traveling through a region of
such vast food resources the Spaniards so often found
themselves starving. One reason for this was that there
were simply too many of them: It takes a lot of food to
feed 50 people 3 square meals a day. And because they

were spending their days outdoors and expending a great deal of energy in strenuous activities, such as building ships and fighting Indians, they were always ravenous. Another reason for the Spaniards' constant hunger was their inability to come to terms with the environment in

The Spaniards passed through regions where the river had flooded and turned the nearby jungle into a tropical swamp. Monstrous "serpents," or anacondas, some of them 25 feet long and as thick as a small tree trunk, swam through these areas.

which they found themselves. They hunted and fished for food and occasionally ventured into the jungle to gather fruit, but these efforts were halfhearted at best. They were predatory men who were accustomed to imposing their will on their surroundings rather than adapting to them. The Indians were not always willing to give food to the intruders, nor were they always willing to trade their food for the useless trinkets the Spaniards offered. The Spaniards would then simply steal food from the Indians instead of going to the trouble of procuring sustenance in a legitimate manner. As the conquistadores were soon to find out, most of the Indians along the Amazon objected to this.

Now that they were on the great river itself, the villages were plentiful on either side. They had entered the territory of Aparia the Greater. The villages they passed were small but the Indians here were friendly and willingly traded fish, turtles, monkeys, parrots, and other food for trinkets. On Sunday, February 26, they were met in the middle of the river by a party of Indians in two canoes. In return for trinkets the Indians offered 10 large turtles, an exchange the Spaniards were delighted to accept. Seeing that the Indians were friendly, and taking pains to be friendly himself, Orellana demonstrated his halting command of their language and struck up a conversation. For weeks he had been hoping to find a village in which they could stay long enough to construct the second boat. For that, friendly relations were all important. Pleased with the conversation conducted in their own tongue with a man of a type and race they had never seen before, the Indians offered to lead the Spaniards to their village, which was farther up the river.

The Indians of Aparia the Greater's settlement gaped at the strange creatures with matted beards, filthy, sunburned skin, and rusty armor. Taking advantage of the effect their arrival produced, Orellana launched into a speech in his pidgin Indian, assuring the Indians that they had no reason

to be afraid. He informed them that he and his companions were Christians who believed in the God who had
created the world; that they were emissaries of the Christian
emperor, King Charles I of Spain; and, taking a page from
Cortés's book, Orellana was careful to add that they were
"children of the sun." This latter statement had the intended effect, for the Indians worshiped the sun and so
took the Spaniards for celestial beings. (Cortés had used
a similar ruse in his conquest of the Aztecs.)

Prompted by Carvajal, Orellana lectured the Indians
and their overlord on the error of worshiping pagan images
and instructed them on the path of Christ. Then, in true
conquistador style, he formally took possession of the village in the name of Spain and planted a large cross in the
center of it. Presumably the Indians did not understand
much of what was going on, for they continued to act
with great hospitality toward the Spaniards, and in fact
offered to provide them with food and to turn the village
over to them for as long as they needed it. Orellana and
"the companions," as Carvajal called the Spaniards, were
overjoyed—they finally had a chance to build the second
boat. (The village's only major drawback was a horrendous
mosquito infestation. According to Carvajal, the mosquitoes were so numerous that while one man ate or worked
on the construction of the boat, another man stood beside
him waving his arms to keep away the voracious, swarming
insects.)

While feasting on the food that the villagers brought to
them every day and listening to the good-natured ha-
rangues of Friar Carvajal (it was Lent, which for Roman
Catholics is normally a time of fasting and penitence),
Orellana's men worked diligently on constructing the new
boat. The men were divided into teams, each assigned
specific tasks. They also repaired the brigantine they had
been traveling in until then, which was rotting badly. (This
may well have been because the wood for the first boat
had been cut at the wrong time. Amazonian Indians cut

As they passed through the rain forest, the Spaniards encountered many animals that were completely alien to them. Their attempts—and those of subsequent explorers—to describe these creatures to artists in Europe resulted in drawings such as this one.

wood from the forest only during the moon's last quarter, believing that wood cut at any other time quickly rots and is eaten by insects. Whether or not the Indians informed the Spaniards of this in time for the building of the second brigantine is not known.)

Within 35 days the new brigantine was finished and the first boat was fully repaired. If it was hard for the conquistadores to forsake the safety and rich diet of the village, the thought of finally escaping its cruel swarms of mosquitoes must have made their departure easier.

There were now two brigantines, and Orellana appointed Cristobal de Segovia, known as Maldonado, a veteran of the conquest, to captain the old ship while he himself took over at the helm of the new one. Alonso de Robles, in whom Orellana apparently placed special confidence, was appointed second-in-command. In the months ahead, Robles would frequently be given the unenviable task of scouting ahead in canoes or on foot with a small group of men while Orellana and the rest of the crew guarded the boats.

The Spanish boats set out from the village of Aparia the Greater on April 24, 1542. They had yet to have any trouble with the Indians. Credit for this goes to Orellana for his superior diplomacy and his ability to learn the various native languages. But the days of a peaceful passage down the Amazon were over, and from here on in the Spaniards were obliged to literally fight their way downriver.

The first Indian encountered outside Aparia the Greater's domain, however, was friendly. Entirely alone, he paddled up to the imposing Spanish boats and allowed himself to be taken aboard. Orellana thought he might prove useful as a guide in the new territory they were entering. But after five days in which the Indian proved to be useless as a guide—he was apparently unaware of the villages that even the Spaniards could see on the riverbanks—he was put back in his canoe and let go.

For two more weeks the Spaniards passed through land that was uninhabited because the river had flooded and the villages along the shore had been abandoned. Nothing of note occurred except for a strange incident involving an iguana and a fish. One of the Spaniards saw an iguana in a tree on the riverbank and took a shot at it with a crossbow. Apparently he was not an experienced crossbowman, for he misloaded it and the crossbow's nut, without which it was useless, fell into the river. This was a major disaster, for the Spaniards had few crossbows to start with and they were absolutely vital to their success in battle. Later that afternoon, however, long after they had resigned themselves to the loss of one of their weapons, someone caught a fish. When the fish was prepared for cooking, the crossbow's nut was found inside its stomach.

Six days later, on May 12, the Spaniards had reason to recall their good fortune. They were now in the domain of Machiparo, who ruled over a warrior tribe that included 50,000 fighting men. According to Carvajal, these warriors were all between the ages of 30 and 70 and sported thin mustaches. The friar described the first encounter with the warriors of Machiparo: "We saw [their] villages glimmering white. We had not proceeded far when we saw

Indian priests, subjects of the overlord Aparia the Greater, gather on a small island in the Amazon River to make offerings to the rising sun. Most of the Indians that Orellana encountered in South America—including the Incas—were sun worshipers.

coming up the river a great many canoes, all equipped for fighting, gaily colored, and [the warriors] with their shields on, which are made out of the shell-like skins of lizards and the hides of manatees and of tapirs, as tall as a man, for they cover them entirely. They were coming on with a great yell, playing on many drums and wooden trumpets, threatening us as if they were going to devour us."

The Spaniards made ready. Orellana ordered the two boats lashed together, halving the number of sides the Indians could attack, and told the crossbowmen and arquebusiers to prepare to open fire. It was then that the arquebusiers discovered that their gunpowder was damp—the guns would not fire. Of the two weapons, crossbow and arquebus, the crossbow was by far the more useful. The inaccurate, scattershot arquebus was more important for its psychological rather than its physical effect on the Indians, who like the Incas had never heard or seen guns before. In terms of loading speed both weapons were slow, but the quicker of the two was the crossbow—it took about a minute and a half to load and fire a single arrow. What made the crossbow even more important to the conquistadores was its chilling accuracy in the hands of a skilled marksman. And Orellana's crossbowmen (except, apparently, the Spaniard who had tried to shoot the iguana) were experts; when they shot they either killed or maimed their victim, and within minutes several of the Indians were dead or wounded. But in Machiparo's warriors the Spaniards had found a persistent foe, and despite the deadly work of the crossbowmen the Indians kept coming.

Orellana ordered his men to row for the village, and some accurate shooting by the crossbowmen allowed a group of the conquistadores to get ashore. Robles scouted the village and found it was heavily and staunchly defended. He returned to Orellana, who was now pinned down on the beach, and informed him of the situation. He also mentioned the abundant food supplies he had seen in the enclave, including pools in which the villagers

fattened their turtles for eating. Orellana immediately ordered Maldonado to take 12 men, reenter the village, and
get the food. This Maldonado attempted to do. Soon however, the 12 Spaniards reemerged, followed by hordes of
enraged Indians. Some of the conquistadores were carrying
fat, live turtles. They managed to get back to their boat
without relinquishing the turtles, but 18 Spaniards were
seriously wounded, and one of them was to die of his
wounds a week later.

They fled downriver with Indian canoes swarming
around them. Machiparo's warriors pursued the intruders
all night long, giving them no respite, and the Spaniards
were unable to eat or sleep. The following day, believing
that they had finally shaken off the pursuit, Orellana and
his men put ashore on a small island so that they might
eat and rest, but once again they were attacked by thousands of Indians, and the chase was on again. Friar Carvajal was particularly unnerved to notice a number of his
counterparts among the attacking hordes: "There were
among these men and the war canoes four or five sorcerers,
all daubed with whitewash and with their mouths full of
ashes, which they blew into the air, having in their hands
a pair of aspergills, with which as they moved along they
kept throwing water about the river as a form of enchant-
ment, and, after they had made one complete turn about
our brigantines . . . they called out to the warriors, and
at once these began to blow their wooden bugles and trumpets and beat their drums and with a very loud yell they
attacked us."

The Indians were relentless and the Spaniards were
growing tired. Finally, Orellana and his men found themselves cornered in a small tributary the Indians had fooled
them into entering. The Indians, having trapped their
quarry, moved in for the kill. What saved the Spaniards—
and not for the last time—was a devastating crossbow shot.
As the Indians glided forward in their canoes, a Spaniard
named Celis, about whom little is known other than this

*On May 12, 1542, Orellana's
men fought their first major
battle with Indians of the
Amazon rain forest. Attacked by
Chief Machiparo's warriors, the
Spaniards were driven ashore and
forced to make a stand. They
eventually escaped with their life
and a number of the Indians'
prize turtles.*

one act, shot the Indians' leader in the chest, killing him
instantly as he stood proudly in his canoe. The Spaniards
were able to take advantage of the Indians' subsequent
confusion and demoralization and slipped back onto the

main branch of the river. They managed to put some distance between themselves and their tormentors, but the Indians followed them downriver for another 48 hours, until they finally passed out of Machiparo's territory.

Amazons

Orellana and his companions had been on the river for five months, and still there was no end in sight. They were now well inside present-day Brazil. Occasionally, friendly Indians were encountered; but when asked about the location of the mouth of the river, the Indians could only respond with blank stares, for most of them had never even considered the possibility that there was an end to the river, and they had no word for such a concept. Orellana might as well have been asking them where the sky ended.

Machiparo's domain had been populous, with large villages that extended in an almost unbroken line for hundreds of miles along the south bank of the river. The territory they were entering now, which was ruled by the overlord Omagua (Machiparo's ally in battles against tribes living farther inland to the south), was equally well inhabited. By this time, the Spaniards could not help but notice that the more developed an Indian village was, the more warlike its inhabitants. Time after time the expedition was forced to steer clear of villages or towns because of the number of warriors standing ready to defend them.

Therefore, the villages the expedition stopped at in Omagua's domain were the smaller ones. The first such village the Spaniards dubbed Pueblo de la Loza, or Porcelainville, for the beauty of the porcelain they found in it. The porcelain was delicately glazed and beautifully painted in vivid

Many of the Indians that the Spaniards encountered during their Amazon odyssey were ferocious; others were hospitable. Some of the Indian villages they visited seemed idyllic, and a number of the weary conquistadores entertained thoughts of abandoning Orellana and settling down with an Indian wife.

colors. There were jars and pitchers large enough to hold 100 gallons, as well as plates, bowls, and candelabra. The villagers offered to take the foreigners inland, where, they claimed, there was more pottery as well as silver and gold in abundance.

Although Orellana did not take the villagers up on their offer, he did make a brief excursion into the rain forest in the company of Robles, Maldonado, Carvajal, and several others. Before they had gone two miles, according to Carvajal, "the roads became more like royal [Spanish] highways and wider." Orellana reluctantly turned back, for such great highways indicated a large population and thus a high risk of being attacked. It is a testament to the battle weariness and general demoralization of the Spaniards that they declined to investigate further, especially in light of the villagers' remarks about the abundance of silver and gold. As far as Orellana knew, these great highways might have led to el Dorado itself. Nevertheless, Orellana ordered his men back to the boats. At this point, his only priority was to get the expedition to the end of the river safely.

By late May 1542 the Spaniards had already passed the river's halfway mark, although there was no way for them to know this. They were now moving through a territory ruled by an overlord named Paguana. The river and the rain forest were beginning to cast a spell over the fatigued explorers. John Hemming, a distinguished historian, has written a vivid description of the region's ambience: "The Amazon here is as broad as a lake, a mass of gently swirling water the color of an Indian's skin. The banks are unbroken lines of dark-green trees masked by a screen of undergrowth. These endless horizons of treetops are broken only by the occasional giant towering above the others, or by banks of mud or sand on which the Indians build their villages. . . . In the sky . . . immense formations of clouds soak up the moisture of the Amazon forests. The clouds pile up or race across the sky, and are reflected in the

waters of the river. At dawn and sunset the surface of the
Amazon mirrors a dazzling spectacle of color, from silver
to orange and deep purple. There is little else to break the
monotony—occasional logs or islands of grasses floating
with the current, a fish breaking the surface, tributaries
or inlets making a brief opening in the walls of trees, or
flights of birds, macaws, herons, or eagles watching the
edges of the river. For most of the time, day after day,
there is only the immensely broad, placid river and the
unbroken lines of trees on its banks."

A strange lassitude befell the Spaniards. Many of them
seemed to be in a fugue state, and they stared dreamily at
the villages that slipped past on the riverbank. Some of

*At the junction of the Amazon
River and the Río Negro, the
Spaniards passed into the domain
of the Amazon woman warriors,
known to other Indians as the
Coniupuyara. Evidence of the
Amazons' wrath—hanging
corpses and severed heads on
posts—lined the riverbanks.*

the men began talking about abandoning the expedition
and seeking permanent refuge in a friendly town. The
men and women in the next village visited by the expedition were so docile that the Spaniards named the spot
Pueblo de los Bobos, or Village of the Idiots. Some of the
Spaniards were loathe to leave this lazy village, and received an indignant lecture from Carvajal, who described

Frightened by the prospect of the Coniupuyara and taunted by other Indians, the Spaniards abandoned what little restraint they still possessed and raided inland villages and temples.

the incident in his journal: "I am telling the truth when I say that there were among us a few so weary of this kind of life and of the long journey that, if their consciences had not kept them from so doing, they would not have failed to remain behind among the Indians." (By "their consciences," Carvajal is referring to himself.) The reluctant conquistadores were finally persuaded to return to the boats. They sailed off with the peaceful villagers' food and several of the Indian women. The women, Carvajal assures us, were taken aboard "to make bread for the companions" and were later released.

The Indians at the next village were not so peaceful.

As the end of the journey drew near, Orellana began to suspect that the local Indians were using poisoned arrows in their attacks on the expedition, and he adopted terror tactics in an attempt to intimidate them.

The Spaniards christened this place Pueblo Vicioso, or
Viciousville, because its numerous inhabitants made it
abundantly clear that they did not want the Spaniards to
stop there. (The names that the Spaniards assigned to the
villages underscore the virulent racism of the Europeans:

If the Indians were peaceful, they were "idiots"; if they defended themselves, they were "vicious.") Carvajal reported that Viciousville had over 500 houses, and that the nearby lands featured large, well-tended orchards in which grew exotic fruits such as custard apples and guavas.

On June 3, they came upon another tributary. Carvajal called it Río Negro (Black River) because of its dark waters, and the name stuck. The friar described the junction of the rivers as a kind of battle between two giants of nature: "We saw the mouth of another great river on the left, which emptied into the one which we were navigating [and] the water of which was black as ink. For this reason we gave it the name of Río Negro, which river flowed so abundantly and with such violence that for more than twenty leagues it formed a streak down through the other water, the one not mixing with the other."

The Spaniards had passed into a new and perilous zone. The first village they visited in this region was notable for the huge wooden idol they discovered there, into which the villagers poured *chicha*, the alcoholic drink they made out of maize, as an offering to the sun. These villagers informed the Spaniards that they were subjects of a great tribe of warrior women, to whom they brought colorful parrot and macaw feathers as tribute. The Indians called these women the Coniupuyara, or "grand mistresses," and feared them greatly. As the Spaniards continued downriver, they began to see tall gibbets to which were nailed "many dead men's heads." This was presumably the work of the Coniupuyara, who the Spaniards had begun to refer to as the Amazons, the female warriors of classic Greek mythology.

Orellana had apparently grown tired of his efforts at diplomacy. Perhaps he and his companions had been unnerved by the heads. The Indians they encountered now mocked them and told them that the Amazons were waiting for them downriver; the Spaniards responded with deadly rage, firing crossbows and arquebuses. When two

(continued on page 81)

Strangers in a Strange Land

Aramilitares *(military macaw)*

Francisco de Orellana and his small band of conquistadores were the first Europeans to penetrate deep into the Amazon rain forest. The warrior-explorers of the Spanish Conquest experienced a wide variety of strange environments during their travels throughout the New World, but none so alien as the tropical jungles of South America. Unlike some of the more sophisticated—and less warlike—European explorers to follow, men of religion and science rather than of empire, the conquistadores were ill prepared to catalog the flora, fauna, and native human inhabitants of this exotic land. (Europe would have to wait until the early 19th century and the South American journeys of the great Alexander von Humboldt for an exhaustive survey of that continent's animal and plant life, and even longer for a good anthropography.) Had one of Orellana's rough crew somehow possessed that ubiquitous 20th-century instrument—the camera—he might have taken photographs much like the following ones.

Toucan

Felispardalis *(ocelot)*

Strelitzia reginae *(bird of paradise flower)*

Yucca

Amazon River fisherman

Amazon River tributary

Floating Indian dwelling

(continued from page 72)

Spaniards were wounded at a village, a captured Indian was later sent back to the village with his back sliced open, and the next morning Orellana hanged several others and burned down their homes. On June 13, Orellana burned alive an entire Indian family in their hut.

The Spaniards were beginning to suspect that some of the Indians were poisoning their arrows, a terrifying prospect. To test this hypothesis, a captured Indian girl was used as a guinea pig. The paste that had been discovered on the enemy arrowheads was rubbed into an incision in her arm. She showed no ill effects, nor seemed to expect any, and the men watching her sighed with relief.

More villages followed. From one, a few canoes floated out. The Indians mystified the Spaniards by repeatedly pointing to the Spaniards' beards and skin and then pointing toward the shore, until it was understood that they were trying to say that there were Europeans living inland from the river. Carvajal found this plausible, but Orellana was unwilling to waste any more time investigating. The expedition was now coming under continual attack, and showers of arrows and sticks rained down on the boats. More than ever before the Spaniards felt like aliens in a hostile world.

Soon after, a group of warriors so flamboyant in their disdain for the Spaniards that Friar Carvajal suspected them of being drunk engaged Orellana's men in a difficult battle. When the conquistadores carried the fight into the village on the riverbank, they saw there "Indian women with bows and arrows who did as much fighting as the Indian men, or even more, and they led on and incited the Indian men to fight; and . . . using the bows and arrows as sticks, would even drub those who started to flee, and they served as captains, commanding those warriors to fight, and placed themselves in the front ranks and held others in position so that they would stand firm in battle, which was entered into very resolutely."

Realizing that this part of his journal might be greeted

with incredulity back in Europe (which indeed it was), Carvajal took pains to "state, by way of clearing myself, that I am talking about something which I actually saw." Adding that the Amazons were so ferocious that they

clubbed to death some of their male comrades who were trying to flee the battle, Carvajal provided a description of the never-to-be-seen-again warrior women: "These women are very white and tall, and have hair very long

Supposedly, the Amazons were fierce warriors who would use captured prisoners for target practice or roast them alive. Orellana's party claimed to have battled the Amazons, who, according to Friar Carvajal, shot so many arrows into the Spaniards' boats that they "looked like porcupines."

An Amazon warrior. An Indian who was familiar with the Amazons assured the Spaniards that any male "who should take it into his head to go down to the country of these women was destined to go a boy and return an old man."

and braided and wound about the head, and they are very robust and go about naked, [but] with their privy parts covered, with their bows and arrows in their hands, doing as much fighting as ten Indian men, and indeed there was one woman among these who shot an arrow a span [about nine inches] deep into one of the brigantines, and others less deep, so that our brigantines looked like porcupines."

Much of what Orellana and his men learned about the Amazons came from an Indian trumpeter they captured during the battle and interrogated. This man stated that he had visited the Amazons in their inland domain frequently. According to him, the Amazons lived in a heavily guarded and partly walled-in city; men were allowed to enter only to pay tribute or to trade. The only other men who entered the Amazons' city were captives from a distant province the Amazons were at war with. These men were brought in for the sole function of procreation. Once the women became pregnant the men were sent away. Male children born to the Amazons were either killed at birth or sent off to join their fathers, whereas females were brought up to be warriors and to live in the same way as their mothers. The Amazons were rich and ruled over all the provinces that surrounded their own. The walls of their homes were decorated with silver, and the upper echelon of Amazons ate from gold plates and wore clothing made of fine wool.

The conquistadores managed to get through the Amazons' territory without losing anybody, but Orellana and Carvajal would never succeed in shaking off their influence. During the fighting, when, according to Carvajal, "arrows were raining down on the boats in such profusion that we could not see each other . . . our Lord permitted [the Amazons], because of my faults, to plant an arrow shot over one of my eyes, the arrow passing through my head and sticking out two fingers' length on the other side behind my ear and slightly above it; from which wound, besides losing my eye, I have endured much suffering and worry."

The Amazons also proved unlucky for Orellana. In Europe, Carvajal's account of their battle with the warrior women captured the imagination of the public more than any other aspect of the journey, and subsequently the river, which was called the Orellana River for a short period, eventually acquired the name by which it is known today.

Deliverance

The grueling cycle continued: The Spaniards proceeded down the river as fast as they could, stopping only to plunder the weaker villages for food and to fight their way through a seemingly endless succession of Indian war parties. The journey had degenerated to the point where such grand words as *conquistador* and *expedition* were no longer appropriate; by now the "conquistadores" were no better than a band of desperate, marauding river pirates, and their "expedition" was no more than a continuous flight from the Indians, who followed inexorably, hoping to teach the intruders a lesson.

Fortunately for the Spaniards (and more so for the Indians) an end to this brutal odyssey was near; about 300 miles from the mouth of the river the first effects of the tidal bore were felt. But any celebration was preempted by another discovery—one the Spaniards had been anticipating with growing dread. In the province they had just entered (ruled, according to the friar, by an overlord named Nurandaluguaburabara) the Indians dipped their arrowheads in a lethal poison known as curare. One Spaniard, Antonio de Carranza, was wounded by an arrow in the foot. It was immediately obvious to Carranza and everybody else that this was no ordinary wound; Carranza's foot and leg quickly turned black as the poison moved up through his body, and he died in agony 24 hours later. The Spaniards spent that night in the forest, where they

While Gonzalo Pizarro was struggling through the jungle toward Quito, his brother Francisco was once again engaged in a deadly feud with the Almagrists. In June 1541 a group of conquistadores led by Diego de Almagro the Younger assassinated Francisco Pizarro in Lima, Peru.

frantically built anti-arrow fortifications for the two boats and attempted to protect themselves with every scrap of material they could find (most of them had discarded their armor long ago). But another Spaniard, Garcia de Soria, was killed by a poisoned arrow during the next river battle. The arrow hardly touched him, falling to the floor of the boat after grazing his thigh. Nevertheless he was dead within 24 hours.

But their tribulations were almost over. In early August 1542, after several more battles (including one with cannibals), the Spaniards came to a halt on an island close to the sea. The Amazon's gigantic mouth (50 miles wide) is full of such islands. Orellana and his men spent three weeks at this place, which they called Starvation Island for obvious reasons. Existing on a diet of snails and crabs, they spent their days scavenging and working to transform the boats into seaworthy craft. Sails were fashioned out of blankets they had stolen from the Indians. Although they lacked anchors, compasses, maps, and any knowledge of how to sail at sea, the Spaniards nevertheless put their trust in these two brigantines—after all, the vessels had brought them safely down the length of the Amazon. They set sail on August 8, and after fighting the Amazon's flood tide for more than two weeks, they were finally delivered from the river's grasp and found themselves on the open sea. All of the Spaniards, including their one-eyed captain, fell to their knees as the one-eyed friar led them in prayers of thanksgiving. Some of the men wept.

Their destination was now Cubagua, an island under Spanish administration that lies 150 miles west of Trinidad. Both ships sailed north along the coast of Brazil. A storm broke during their third night on the Atlantic, and the two little vessels were tossed about like pieces of driftwood. When dawn arrived Orellana could not see the other boat. Assuming that it had been sunk during the storm, the surviving Spaniards grieved. Orellana especially was heartbroken to have come so far and through such peril only to lose half his company within days of journey's end. But when they arrived at Cubagua they were greeted, to their amazement and joy, by their missing comrades. The storm had neither wrecked their vessel nor drowned the men. Rather, it had driven their lighter craft miles ahead of Orellana's, and they had arrived at Cubagua first. The date of Orellana's arrival was September 11, 1542. They had departed Quito 18 months before.

While celebrating their deliverance in the town of Nueva Cadiz on Cubagua, Orellana and his companions wondered about the fate of Gonzalo Pizarro and the main party of conquistadores they had left behind in the rain forest so long ago. And Gonzalo Pizarro, for his part, was thinking of Orellana; he had recently sent a letter regarding

Orellana's men feared capture by hostile Indian tribes, who were known to inflict great cruelties on their prisoners. Here, Indians teach a conquistador a harsh lesson concerning the Spanish thirst for gold by pouring molten gold down his throat, while others dismember, cook, and eat their captives.

Gonzalo Pizarro emerged from the rain forest in June 1542 only to be told of his brother Francisco's murder. According to witnesses, the 63-year-old governor of Peru defended himself with vigor, killing one of his assailants before being struck down by numerous blows. His mangled body was quickly buried in an unmarked grave.

his former lieutenant to the king of Spain. In this letter, Pizarro leveled charges of mutiny and treason at Orellana, claiming that Orellana had deserted him and left his company to languish in the rain forest while he (Orellana) went on to fame and glory as the first man to navigate the Amazon.

In an Amazonian sentence, an indignant Pizarro expressed his feelings on the matter: "Paying no heed to what he [Orellana] owed to the services of Your Majesty and to what it was his duty to do as he had been told by me, his captain, and to the well-being of the expeditionary force and of the enterprise, instead of bringing the food [ostensibly, Orellana had gone ahead to locate food or friendly villages where food could be obtained], he went down the river without leaving any arrangements, leaving only the signs and choppings showing how they had been on land and had stopped at the junction of the rivers and at other parts, without there having come in any news of him at all up to the present time; he thus displaying toward the whole expeditionary force the greatest cruelty that ever faithless men have shown, aware that it was left so unprovided and caught in such a vast uninhabited region and among such great rivers, carrying off all the arquebuses and crossbows and munitions and iron materials of the whole expeditionary force."

Orellana's achievement in navigating the Amazon was remarkable, and it can only be viewed as one of the great journeys in the history of exploration. But his accomplishment and reputation would be permanently tainted by Pizarro's accusations. The issue has been debated by historians ever since, with the majority coming down on the side of Pizarro and condemning Orellana. Did Orellana deliberately desert Pizarro and his men in order to claim the glory of the Amazon for himself? No. Orellana made the only logical choice under the circumstances. To travel back upriver, through a hostile environment, with his men already in a weakened condition, was a virtual impossibility. (If anybody in the entire episode remains open to charges of treason and mutiny, it is Orellana's men. The "petition" they presented to Orellana at the village of Aparia the Lesser, in which they implored their captain not to attempt a return journey upriver because that would be "furnishing an occasion for our disobeying Your Worship," was a thinly veiled, and mutinous, threat. Orellana chose wisely not to interpret it as such, and one can only wonder how the savage Gonzalo Pizarro would have reacted to it.)

If Pizarro was in a foul mood when he wrote his letter to the king, it is understandable. He was still recovering from the disastrous attempt to locate el Dorado. After Orellana and his company had gone ahead in search of food, Pizarro's situation had degenerated into a waking nightmare. After waiting 12 days for Orellana to return, Pizarro and his party then advanced to the junction of the Napo and the Amazon, where they saw signs of Orellana, but no Orellana. With no boats and their food supply almost exhausted, they had no choice but to attempt a retreat. Nothing Orellana and his comrades suffered during their journey downriver compared to the horrors experienced by Pizarro's party as they attempted to walk out of the rain forest.

Pizarro led them in the general direction of Quito, and for nine months the Spaniards hacked their way through the tangled underbrush. Sometimes it rained for weeks on end. Their clothing rotted; so did their skin. Wracked by disease and starvation, there were times when the Spaniards literally crawled through the jungle. While the horses were still alive, Pizarro and his men obtained meals by slicing chunks from the starving animals' sides as they walked along and then dressing the wounds in mud. Periodically, they would drain the horses' blood to turn into a soup, which they boiled inside their helmets, seasoning it with pepper and herbs. Once the horses were gone, the conquistadores began to cast greedy eyes on any member

Spanish colonists hunting Indian slaves. The Spanish colonial slave system in Peru, known as the encomienda, *enabled many colonists to maintain a relatively privileged standard of living. But the New Laws of the Indies, passed in November 1542, placed constraints on the encomienda.*

of the party who seemed to be near death. They waited hungrily for their countrymen to expire.

It was a ghastly parade that Gonzalo Pizarro led into Quito in June 1542. Many of the Quitans fled at the sight of this procession of naked, filthy, emaciated men, fearing that they were the walking dead. Of the more than 4,000 people who had set out on the expedition, only 80 returned. These wretched survivors stumbled about the town looking for food. The townspeople, learning who these broken men were, began to feed them. Some of the Spaniards ate so much during their first meal that their shrunken stomachs ruptured and they died.

For Gonzalo Pizarro there was no rest, for bad news greeted him in Quito: Francisco Pizarro had been assassinated almost a year earlier by the followers of the same Almagro faction that the Pizarros had defeated in the civil war of 1538. While Gonzalo Pizarro had been hacking his way through the rain forest, Diego de Almagro the Younger had proclaimed himself king of Peru, a treasonous act in the eyes of Spain. Gonzalo's sole stroke of fortune was that his reemergence in Quito coincided with the arrival of the king's emissary from Spain, sent to Peru with orders to gather a royalist army and put down the Almagrist rebels. Only too happy to avenge his brother's death, Pizarro joined the royalist forces and, fighting with the customary Pizarro ruthlessness and savagery, helped them crush the rebellion.

One month later, in November 1542, the New Laws of the Indies were passed in Spain. The New Laws limited the conquistadores' powers over the native Indian population in Peru, particularly in regard to the keeping of Indians as slaves. Most of the Inca gold and silver had long ago been melted down into bars and shipped back to Spain or had disappeared into the roomy pockets of the conquistadores themselves, and now the practice of holding Indian slaves, known as the *encomienda*, had become a major source of wealth for the Spanish colonists. (The

slaves also sweetened considerably the colonists' life-style.)
A fierce debate over the morality of the encomienda and
the conquest itself sprang up in Spain. (The debate was
initiated and led primarily by Roman Catholic orders such
as the Dominicans and the Jesuits. Friar Carvajal was to
become a leading figure in this movement.) The result
was the New Laws, which sought to protect the rights of
the native South Americans.

To conquistadores, such as Gonzalo Pizarro, the new
legislation was an affront to their dignity and freedom.
They had conquered Peru, not the pampered moralizers
in Spain. Their anger soon turned into widespread rebellion, and now it was Pizarro's turn to lead an insurrection
against the Crown. In September 1544 he entered the city
of Lima on horseback, fully recovered from his ordeal in
the rain forest and no longer in rags but arrayed in all the
finery of a legendary conquistador. The royalist viceroy
was sent packing and Gonzalo Pizarro crowned himself
king of Peru. His reign was short but characteristically
bloody. Pizarro's experience in the rain forest had not
taught him humility; within 2 years of his coronation he
had executed 340 of his fellow Spaniards and countless
Indians for various crimes of disloyalty and treason. It is
lucky for Orellana that he remained outside of Pizarro's
grasp during this period.

Although still professing loyalty to Spain, Pizarro had
effectively established a rival dynasty. This was a development that the king of Spain could not fail to act on. In
1546 the deposed viceroy returned to Peru, this time bringing with him royal documents amending some of the con-
troversial New Laws so they would be more favorable to
the conquistadores. Threatened with open rebellion and
loss of the revenue the colonies brought him, the king had
decided to sacrifice the rights of the Indians to his own
pressing political and financial needs. Pizarro had now lost
the moral basis on which he had originally staked his
rebellion—protecting his colonial *compadres* from the

"unfair" New Laws. His supporters began to defect to the royalist camp. The viceroy lost his first battle with Pizarro in October 1547, but in the next major battle, Pizarro saw 45 of his most loyal supporters killed and watched helplessly as the rest of his army deserted him for the other side. He himself was captured and promptly executed. The two great and bloody Pizarros, Francisco and Gonzalo, were dead. Like Inca Atahualpa before them, they died violently at the hands of Spanish executioners.

On April 9, 1548, Gonzalo Pizarro's supporters faced royalist forces and their Indian allies outside Cuzco. It was Gonzalo's last stand; his army was crushed and he was captured and put to death.

"To Come to a Land of Christians"

Almost all of Orellana's men left Cubagua not long after their arrival and returned to Peru to fight with or against Gonzalo Pizarro. Friar Carvajal also returned to Peru, having heard that his mentor, Bishop Valverde, had been killed during an Indian uprising on Puná, an island off the coast of Ecuador. Despite the horrible injury he had suffered during the passage down the Amazon, Carvajal enjoyed a long and rewarding life after he parted company with Orellana. Widely respected and liked, he became an advocate of Indian rights and died peacefully at the age of 80 in a Lima monastery.

Orellana himself, still unaware of Pizarro's letter to the king, prepared to return to Spain and to reap the rewards of his labors. No doubt he would be received with much fanfare, and surely his days as a middling conquistador were now over. Perhaps the king would make him a governor or put him in charge of an important new expedition.

On the voyage home Orellana was accompanied by Maldonado, the only member of the crew to return to Europe with him. Before reaching Spain they stopped in Lisbon, Portugal. They stayed there for two weeks, enjoying the hospitality of the Portuguese king, who was eager to hear the details of their historic voyage. Impressed by what Orellana had to relate, the king offered to finance a second expedition. Orellana turned the offer down and

The spirits of Hope and Fame lavish their attentions on explorer Christopher Columbus. Francisco de Orellana, even after his Amazon River ordeal, continued to hear the call of these two Sirens, who lured him to his death in 1545.

continued on to Spain with Maldonado. Having been offered financial backing by a foreign monarch for a second
expedition, and having refused it out of loyalty to his own
king and country, he felt sure that Charles I would reward
him generously.

He was wrong. Orellana arrived in Spain in May 1543,
but his account of the voyage down the great river did not
win him the high praise and renown he had imagined.
One reason for this was Pizarro's letter, which cast a
shadow over the entire enterprise. The Pizarros had many
allies in Spain, and they did their best to discredit Orellana.
Orellana's stay in Portugal, which at the time was Spain's
great rival, and his frank conversations with the Portuguese
king were also frowned upon, because there was some
confusion and contention as to whether the Amazon's
mouth actually fell in Spanish or Portuguese colonial territory.

Nevertheless, Orellana petitioned the king to authorize
and finance a new expedition to the Amazon. Despite the
travails he had already suffered in South America, Orellana was anxious to return. Soon his desire to once again
see the great river became an obsession. Perhaps Orellana
believed he could clear his name and achieve the honor
he sought by undertaking another great journey. Or perhaps it was simply his conquistador's blood that spurred
him on. Whatever his reasons, the Spaniard was willing
to sacrifice everything to return to that savage green world.

Nine months went by before Orellana learned whether
his petition was to be granted. Finally he received word
that the king had authorized a new expedition. Orellana
was given the title of *adelantado* (governor) and the rank
of captain general, and was authorized to colonize and
further explore the land south of the Amazon River to the
distance of 200 leagues. He was instructed to take with
him 200 infantrymen, 100 horsemen, and the material
out of which 2 riverboats could be constructed. He was
also to take eight friars (to spread the Catholic religion

among the natives), eight black slaves, and an "inspector general"—in reality, a government overseer who would report back to the king on Orellana's activities. Once he arrived at the Amazon, this time entering it from the Atlantic, Orellana was to build two towns, one of which would be situated at the river's mouth. How much money did the king grant to Orellana to finance such a massive venture? None. He was to raise the money for the expedition out of his own pocket.

Insulted and disappointed, but not defeated, Orellana traveled to Seville, in southern Spain, and set to work. He was nothing if not dogged. Soon he discovered that if he was going to launch a second expedition there was more to overcome than a lack of funding. The two things (aside from money) that Orellana most needed were bluntly refused him at the outset: He was forbidden either to hire a Portuguese pilot (this was vital, as there were no Spanish pilots familiar with the Brazilian coast), or to press (force) unemployed sailors into accompanying him on his journey, as was common practice at the time.

Other, more insidious problems vexed Orellana. His efforts to mount the expedition were blocked mysteriously at every turn. There was, as Orellana himself put it in a letter to the king, "a worm in our midst." The worm, or worms, seemed to be all over Seville, speaking to everyone Orellana spoke to, shadowing his every move and ruining all his plans. No sooner had Orellana found a backer than the backer's offer was inexplicably withdrawn, sometimes within hours of the original agreement. Merchants who had formerly been happy to accept payments on credit suddenly insisted on being paid in cash. Men who had enthusiastically asked to take part in the expedition changed their mind overnight, and no amount of persuasion could bring them round to their original position.

Who was the worm? Orellana's most obvious enemies were the Pizarros and their supporters in Spain, who believed that Orellana had betrayed Gonzalo Pizarro. Only

A map of the New World drawn at the end of the 16th century shows the extent—as well as the limit—of European knowledge of New World geography during the waning years of the Spanish conquest.

one of the Pizarros, Hernando, was in Spain at the time. He was in jail, but according to those who saw him there, his prison was more like a palace. He drew money from his estates in Peru and was allowed the company of a 17-year-old wife. Although he was imprisoned, he might easily have used his considerable wealth and influence to ensure that Orellana's second expedition was a failure.

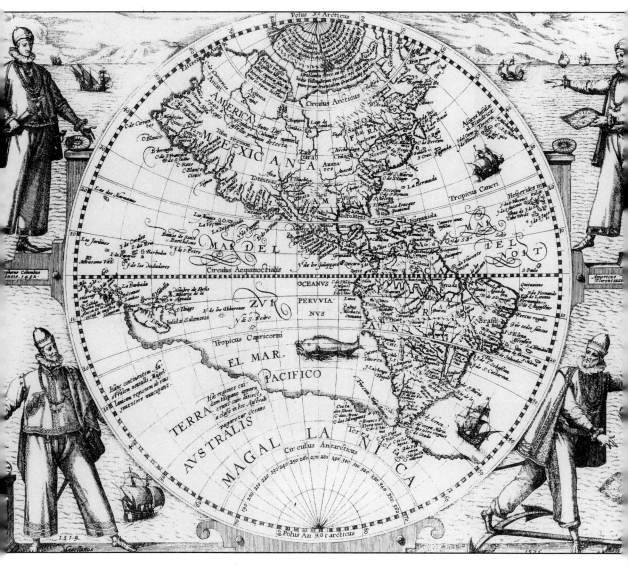

There are other candidates for the treachery that undermined Orellana's enterprise, among them the Portuguese, who had good reason to prevent the Spaniard from returning to South America. The territory at the mouth of the Amazon was in dispute. If Orellana was successful in building a Spanish town there, as King Charles had instructed him, it would give the Spanish a solid foothold in the area. And a Portuguese agent had been spotted in Seville, apparently hoping to persuade some of Orellana's men to join a Portuguese expedition.

The most intriguing possibility of all, however, is Maldonado, Orellana's sole remaining companion from his previous expedition. Apparently their friendship did not survive long in Seville. According to the king's inspector general, there was open dissension between the two men, with "secret and sly factions" springing up on Maldonado's side. Maldonado later joined forces with the Portuguese. In a letter to the king, the inspector general wrote that one of Orellana's former companions had fled to Portugal "because he had been involved in the slaying of a man here in Seville." This must have been Maldonado, who was the only member of the first expedition in Europe and who had been with Orellana in Lisbon when the Portuguese offer to finance a second expedition had been made. Having quarreled with his former commander and having been forced to flee his native Spain, Maldonado had at least two good reasons to sabotage Orellana.

Surprisingly, Orellana's most staunch and influential ally turned out to be the inspector general, Friar Pablo de Torres. Torres sympathized with Orellana. At this point the conquistador's obsession had made him into an almost pathetic figure. The friar wrote that Orellana was "so kind-hearted that every time a person tells him something he believes it and acts on it, and so much gentleness at times is of little profit to one." Discussing Orellana's crippling lack of funds, and the government's failure to supply any, Friar Torres wrote, "I beseech Your Majesty, since up to now this enterprise has been so completely deprived of recognition and so utterly ignored, to take a more personal interest in it from now on, and that Your Majesty will bestow upon it some more special favor."

But no "special favor" was forthcoming. Orellana simply muddled onward. His obsession was all consuming. He was perhaps a bit mad by this time, for his view of the situation was wildly unrealistic. He had accepted the king's conditions on February 18, 1544, five days after they had been offered to him and almost a year after his arrival in Spain. By May he was already announcing his imminent departure, even though he had neither paid for his two ships nor managed to recruit the number of sailors required. October arrived and he still had not sailed, and some of those who had originally intended to travel with him had already left on other ships. In November, Orellana further complicated the situation by suddenly deciding to marry a very young, very poor girl, Ana de Ayala. Friar Torres must have groaned upon hearing this news. He had already written to the king informing him that "people are approaching the Adelantado here with marriage proposals," a development that pleased the friar greatly—if Orellana could find himself a wife of good family with a sizable dowry his financial problems might be resolved in an instant. "May Your Majesty be informed," an appalled Friar Torres later wrote, "that the Adelantado has married, despite my attempts to persuade him [not to], which were many and well founded, because they did not give him any dowry whatsoever, I mean not a single ducat."

And yet, amazingly, Orellana's ships finally set sail. The two vessels left Spain on May 11, 1545, a full year after he had first announced his departure. They embarked illegally, against the express orders of the king; the condition of Orellana's vessels and crew had repeatedly failed to pass the inspections of government officials. Orellana took to the seas nevertheless, in effect cutting himself off

from Spain, which he would never lay eyes on again. He took his new bride with him.

Long before it even reached the Brazilian coast, the second expedition had become a disaster. Hoping to procure some of the provisions he had been unable to get in Seville, Orellana spent three months on the Canary Islands and two months on the Cape Verde Islands, both off the northwest coast of Africa. During this time he lost 98 men to sickness; another 50, believing Orellana to be insane and inept, deserted. When he finally set sail again, one of his 2 ships, carrying another 77 people, a riverboat, and several horses, disappeared in mid-Atlantic and was never seen again.

With what remained of his expedition Orellana finally returned to the mouth of the river that had taken such an unshakable hold on his thoughts. Orellana maneuvered his ship slowly upstream through the myriad tributaries and islands at the Amazon's mouth, stopping only to gather food and timber to build another riverboat. By this point the expedition was clearly doomed. Orellana refused to turn back. Sixty more people died, falling prey to Indians, starvation, and disease. To make matters worse, the ship was driven ashore and beached on a small island.

Along with his daily dose of disaster, Orellana had been forced to swallow a singular, maddening irony: He had been unable to locate the main branch of the river that was his sole claim to fame. Approaching the Amazon's

In 16th-century Spain, the Roman Catholic junta wielded significant political influence and often functioned as an arm of the state. King Charles I appointed Friar Pablo de Torres royal overseer on Orellana's second— and final—expedition.

enormous mouth on the Atlantic instead of following it down from its headwaters in Peru, he was at a loss to find the main body of the river among the maze of islands and tributaries that clutter its entrance. It was as if he had never seen the river before. He had been drawn across the ocean to the Amazon once again only to be unable to find it.

According to one of the survivors, a feverish Orellana now declared that "he had made up his mind to come to a land of Christians." He set off from the island with a small crew in a newly built brigantine. His wife and the other remaining members of the expedition waited on the island. Orellana never found his land of Christians or the main body of the Amazon River. He returned to the island almost a month later, having lost to the Indians 17 of the men who had gone with him. His wife and the other castaways were gone; they had pieced together a small boat out of the larger wrecked one and had sailed out of the river and up the Brazilian coast to the island of Margarita. According to one of the men who was with him and who eventually made it back to civilization, the exhausted Orellana, upon returning to the island and finding his wife and comrades gone, simply sat down within sight of the rushing water and passed quietly away.

The doomed Francisco de Orellana spent his final days in a small, improvised boat much like this one, hopelessly lost among the islands at the mouth of the Amazon River.

Further Reading

Carvajal, Gaspar de. *Discovery of the Amazon According to the Accounts of Friar Gaspar de Carvajal and Other Documents.* New York: AMS Press, 1964.

Cousteau, Jacques-Yves, and Mose Richards. *Jacques Cousteau's Amazon Journey.* New York: Abrams, 1984.

Gibson, Charles. *Spain in America.* New York: HarperCollins, 1968.

Goulding, Michael. *The Fishes and the Forest: Exploration in Amazonian Natural History.* Berkeley: University of California Press, 1981.

Haring, Clarence H. *The Spanish Empire in America.* San Diego: Harcourt Brace Jovanovich, 1963.

Hemming, John. *The Conquest of the Incas.* San Diego: Harcourt Brace Jovanovich, 1970.

Holdstock, Robert. *The Emerald Forest.* New York: NY Zoetrope, 1985.

Jordan, C. F., ed. *Amazonian Rain Forests.* New York: Springer-Verlag, 1986.

Markham, Clements R., ed. *Expeditions in the Valley of the Amazons.* New York: Ben Franklin, 1964.

Means, Philip A. *Fall of the Inca Empire and the Spanish Rule in Peru, 1530–1780.* New York: Gordian, 1964.

Medina, Jose T. *The Discovery of the Amazon.* New York: Dover, 1988.

Parry, John H. *Spanish Seaborne Empire.* New York: Knopf, 1966.

Stefansson, Vilhjalmur. *Great Adventures and Explorations.* New York: Dial Press, 1947.

Towle, George M. *Pizarro: His Adventures and Conquest.* Boston: Lathrop, Lee, & Shepard, 1898.

Chronology

Entries in roman refer to events directly relating to Francisco de Orellana and the exploration of the Amazon River; entries in italics refer to important cultural and historical events of the era.

1518	*Hernán Cortés conquers the Aztecs in Mexico*
1527	*Spanish ships commanded by Francisco Pizarro encounter a band of Incas on a raft off the Pacific coast of present-day Ecuador*
1530	*Pizarro receives permission from the Spanish crown to organize a full-scale expedition of conquest against the Incas*
1532	*Pizarro begins his march into Peru; attacks the city of Cajamarca with an army of 160 and overcomes more than 5,000 Incas without suffering one fatal casualty; takes the Inca Atahualpa prisoner*
1533	*Accepts more than $6 million in gold from the Incas for the release of Atahualpa but has him killed nonetheless*
1534–40	Francisco de Orellana and Gonzalo Pizarro (Francisco's half brother) make names for themselves in the war for Spanish supremacy in South America; Orellana is appointed lieutenant governor of Puertoviejo by Francisco Pizarro; Gonzalo Pizarro is named governor of the province of Quito
Feb.–Dec. 1541	Gonzalo Pizarro leads his great army from Quito in search of the mythical el Dorado; as the Spaniards hack their way through the dense jungle, the search for the golden city is reduced to a fight for mere survival; Orellana volunteers to take a party of men down the Napo River to locate badly needed food and supplies
Dec. 1541	Orellana and his men reach the village of Imara where they spend a month eating and resting; decide to forge ahead rather than travel back to meet Pizarro who was, by then, some 700 miles away

Feb. 1542	Orellana's party reaches the Amazon River; are feasted at a village of friendly Indians, where they build a second boat but soon wear out their welcome
May–Aug. 1542	While traveling the Amazon through the domains of Machiparo, Omagua, and the Coniupuyara, a band of warrior women, the expedition is attacked and harrassed relentlessly; it finally reaches Starvation Island, at the mouth of the Amazon
Sept. 1542	Orellana and his men arrive at Cubagua, a Spanish-controlled island 150 miles west of Trinidad
1543	Returns to Spain, where he is greeted with contempt because of a letter written to the king by Gonzalo Pizarro claiming that Orellana had left him to languish in the rain forest
1544	Pizarro overthrows the Spanish authorities and crowns himself king of Peru; Orellana given permission to undertake another journey to the Amazon, but must finance it himself; efforts to fund the journey are dogged by supporters of Pizarro
1545	Orellana's ships finally set sail for the Amazon; Orellana loses one of his ships and many of his men in the cross-Atlantic journey; reaches the mouth of the river but cannot locate the main artery in a maze of islands and tributaries; deserted by his wife and his remaining crew, he crawls into a thicket and dies

Index

Brendan Bernhardt has an M.A. from Cambridge University in England. He is a freelance writer and currently resides in Greenwich Village, in New York City.

William H. Goetzmann holds the Jack S. Blanton, Sr., Chair in History at the University of Texas at Austin, where he has taught for many years. The author of numerous works on American history and exploration, he won the 1967 Pulitzer and Parkman prizes for his *Exploration and Empire: The Role of the Explorer and Scientist in the Winning of the American West, 1800–1900*. With his son William N. Goetzmann, he coauthored *The West of the Imagination*, which received the Carr P. Collins Award in 1986 from the Texas Institute of Letters. His documentary television series of the same name received a blue ribbon in the history category at the American Film and Video Festival held in New York City in 1987. A recent work, *New Lands, New Men: America and the Second Great Age of Discovery*, was published in 1986 to much critical acclaim.

Michael Collins served as command module pilot on the *Apollo 11* space mission, which landed his colleagues Neil Armstrong and Buzz Aldrin on the moon. A graduate of the United States Military Academy, Collins was named an astronaut in 1963. In 1966 he piloted the *Gemini 10* mission, during which he became the third American to walk in space. The author of several books on space exploration, Collins was director of the Smithsonian Institution's National Air and Space Museum from 1971 to 1978 and is a recipient of the Presidential Medal of Freedom.

Picture Credits

DATE DUE